A Poet Is A Poet
No Matter How Tall

Poems by poets of all shapes and sizes

Edited by Raundi K. Moore-Kondo

Copyright © 2013 Raundi K. Moore-Kondo
Cover Art by Alexis Tan
Cover Design by Cheng Cheng Tan

Ants and *Sandwich* First published in I Am My Own Orange County: Selected Writings: 1990-1997, Ain't Got No Press

Cows On The Freeway, First Published in: Pearl, Spring, 1994 Also Published in: Cows on the Freeway, iUniverse Press

My Kidney Just Arrived At LAX, First published in My Kidney Just Arrived, Tebot Bach, 2011

The Color of Cody First published in Omnivore

ISBN-13: 978-0615881638 (For The Love Of Words)
ISBN-10: 0615881637

For the Love of the
Two Idiots who peddle my kind of poetry—
Ben Trigg & Steve Ramirez

Thinking kids
by Martha Jeanne Stothard

You've heard it said "Kids should be seen and not heard."
Well I think that is completely absurd.
Kids might be small but they have lots on their mind.
They're thinking great thoughts of every kind.

A Poet is a Poet No Matter How Tall

Poems by poets of all shapes and sizes

Editor's note / 15

Mike Lemp / 16
Raundi Wants a Poem

Lydia Quevedo / 17
How to Cook a Haiku

Ben Trigg / 18
Grocery List

Luke Salazar / 19
The Art of Using Writer's Blocks to Build Something

Graham Smith / 20
Haiku

Don Kingfisher Campbell / 21
The World Is

Carrie McKay / 23
The Detective is In

Rick Lupert / 24
Ants

Shelby Hayes / 25
Insanely Bloodthirsty

Steve Ramirez / 26
The Zombie Cheesecake

Michael Cantin / 27
Morning Tutelage with Alestair

Seth Halbeisen / 29
Vaya con Queso

Rick Lupert / 31
Sandwich

Lauren / 33
Pedro: The Taco Stylist

Leanne Hunt / 34
The Unicyclists' Union Votes are In

Raundi K. Moore-Kondo / 35
I Am a Parrot in a Cage

RD Armstrong / 37
What Unites Us

Graham Smith / 38
Haiku

Matt Foster / 39
Tall

Leslie Maryann Neal / 40
The Apple Never Falls Far from the Tree-- She Jumps

Alexis Tan / 41
The Fall That Never Came

Anahita Amirshahi / 42
The Anticipation of Winter

Vanessa / 43
Gingerbread House

Lena / 45
Spring

Noor Bashir / 46
My Seasons

Eric Lawson / 47
When the Cows Come Home

G. Murray Thomas / 49
Cows On The Freeway

Alexis Tan / 50
Rainbow Fish

Darian Agredano / 51
Nibble... Nibble...   CHOMP!!!

Lena / 52
Shells

Leslie Maryann Neal / 53
Mermaid

Andy Buell / 54
Fish Tank Diver

Anahita Amirshahi / 55
Jerome

Maggie G. Brown / 57
Shape Shifter

Andy Buell / 59
A Bored Ghost

Cynthia Quevedo / 60
Bluebeard Wears Tommy Bahama

Ken Schmidt / 61
My Shadow

Ralph R. Moore / 63
Suwannee

Ralph R. Moore / 65
Suwannee

Annelise Cramm / 66
Laughs

Karina Cramm / 67
Ode To Rotten Banana Peel

JL Martindale / 68
Fountain of My Youth

Annelise Cramm / 69
Nighttime

Vanessa / 70
Fairy Doll

Kelsey Bryan Zwick / 71
jacaranda song

Darian Agredano / 73
The park

Ruth Blue / 74
Robot Robot

Steve Ramirez / 75
Before We Knew It Was Episode IV

Karina Cramm / 76
My Room

Ben Trigg / 77
Hiding

Heather Autumn Love / 78
Why, As a Child, I Hated Taking Grandma to the Bus Depot

Peggy Dobreer 80
Somniloquy, by which I Mean Parasomnia

Jaimes Palacio / 81
Burning Down The Stars

Lydia Quevedo / 83
Softly Through the Night

Cassy Agredano / 88
To be a dancer

Stefano Capobiano / 89
Be (What You Dream)

Maggie G. Brown / 90
A World in a Dream

Raundi K. Moore-Kondo / 92
Sweetest Dreams

Lori McGinn / 94
Emma had a Monet dream

Peggy Dobreer / 95
Nhhhhhh

Ricki Mandeville / 96
Nights I Can't Sleep, I Ride

Angela Moore / 97
Sweet Dreams

Jaimes Palacio / 98
Donut Part 2

Angela Moore / 99
Blue Heron

Khadija Anderson / 100
Cooper Creek

Julia Beasley / 101
Blue Jay!

Carrie McKay / 102
Sequoia Immigration Studies

Lori McGinn / 103
Half-Dome

Stefano Capobianco / 105
True Love

Emma McGinn / 106
Love Is…

Satyajit Mayadas / 107
I love you more then anything

Maggie Ambrose / 108
A Love Poem

Adem Oygur / 109
The Chicken and the Mouse

Nursultan Oygur / 110
Planting a Garden

JL Martindale / 111
Aunt Otter's Garden

Ken Schmidt / 112
Oohhhh, I get it

Emme O'Toole / 114
A Journal's Entry

Maggie Ambrose / 115
Four Chickens in a Coop

Omer Oygur / 116
The Bird is Flying

Benci Udovch Gottdank / 117
The Interesting Pretending Objects

Satyajit Mayadas / 118
The Round Rainbow Bubble

Kathryn Claudi-Magnussen / 119
What color am I?

Daniel McGinn / 121
The Color of Cody

Luke Salazar / 123
Mother

Nicholas Stephen / 124
Collective Epiphanies

Emme O'Toole / 127
I am the Title of your Book

G. Murray Thomas / 128
"Your Kidney Just Arrived At Lax"

Eric Lawson / 130
Airplane Cruises Towards a Crack in the Window Pane

Martha Jeanne Stothard / 131
The Lonely Moon

Nursultan Oygur / 132
Queen of The Clouds

Ella Hayes / 133
I Am A Black Cat

Neela / 134
Rock Star Cheetah

Collin Moore / 135
Do I Remember...

Alison / 136
The Riddler

Matt Foster / 137
The Impossible

Michael Cantin / 138
Cretaceous Carnivore, Cantankerous

Greg Patrick / 139
Dragon's Own. To Usurp the Night's Throne

Khadija Anderson / 142
Super Chief

Ricki Mandeville / 143
My Father's Hands

Stephanie Jones / 144
He never did

Seth Halbeisen / 145
Sadness is Bad

Betsy Mars / 146
Inflammatory

Daniel McGinn / 148
Now that I'm Sixty

Thea Iberall / 149
The recipe

RD Armstrong / 151
Corizon

Cynthia Quevedo / 152
But For A Home

Ruth Blue / 153
Mind

Thea Iberell / 154
Orejas de Elephante

Betsy Mars / 155
Pole Dancing

Don Kingfisher Campbell / 156
The World Is

Nicholas Steffen / 158
Distance

Leanne and Katie Hunt / 159
Mother and Daughter Acrostics Fly across Sky and Kitchen Table

Stephanie Jones / 160
Rest

Acknowledgements / 162

Editors Note:

Raundi wants a poem...

It's true. I do, for there is nothing I love better than a good back-story. To me the "poem" is the greatest artistic form a back-story can take, as it always seeks to convey the author's highest and deepest truth. I find that the more fictional a poem is, the more truth it tells. In that way poems help me to fall more in love with people and words, everyday.

The poets featured in this all-ages anthology range from age 5 to 89, and they happen to be some of the bravest people I know. Each of them is a superhero revealing a few of their secret powers. They know that you don't have to be a super tall or Tony Stark rich with an iron suit to make the world a more lovable place. You don't even have to have an MFA. You only need a voice that you are willing to share.

Thank you to all of my fellow poets and fans of poetry for making my anthology dreams come true. I finally own a poetry book I can share with everyone. I hope you enjoy it as much as I do.

For the love of words,
Raundi K. Moore-Kondo

P.S. Send me a poem. I'll read it, and I might even put it in a book.

www.theloveofwords.com

Poems by poets of all shapes and sizes

Mike Lemp

Raundi Wants a Poem

Raundi wants a poem,
She wants it right away.
If I'd known it was so urgent,
I'd have started yesterday.
I just need something easy
To say in a short time
Should it be intellectual,
Or just have words that rhyme?
Every story has a moral,
And this one has one too.
Be kind to everybody,
So they will be kind too!

Lydia Quevedo

How to Cook a Haiku

Bring the following ingredients
to room temperature
before cooking:
a moment,
a simple observation,
a pack of every word that you know in all languages
preferably pre-coated with calmness,
and a seventeen-syllable mold.
Select words that suit the observation
and compliment the moment, as many
as will fit the mold
without cramping.
Stir vigorously until the words
are where you want them.
Let cook on a 360 degree
page
for ten to fifteen minutes,
stirring occasionally.
The haiku will be very delicate
but very powerful in image.
Serves
more than six billion people.

Ben Trigg

Grocery List

Milk, one gallon
Bread, whole wheat
Apples, Granny Smith, five
Ice cream the flavor of fire against the roof of your mouth, 2 pints
Cereal, any brand, must be in the shape of wagon wheels, handlebars,
or otherwise be evocative of transportation
Frozen dinners with penguins on the box
Six pack of carbonated sorrow
Sunrise
One pound ground beef

Don't forget coupons

Luke Salazar

The Art of Using Writer's Blocks to Build Something
for Doc

I'd been pondering, planning, preparing my poem
I'd wrangled with rhythm and written down rhymes,
I'm finally ready to get it all down,
Obtained some sweet silence and bartered some time.

I gathered my notes and I brewed me a cup
And went to go fetch that new notepad of mine,
The one with the Cat in the Hat on the front,
The one that I now, for some reason, can't find.

Cat in the Hat pad, O where did you go?
I saw it just last weekend, that much I know.
It's stuck in my head now, that till you are found,
This poem of mine just won't get off the ground!

I ripped up my bedroom, I looked everywhere,
And I yelled and I cussed and I tore at my hair
But I finally mumbled (though it was a sting)
"Get a grip on yourself, fool, and *write* the damned thing."

It's funny, the different excuses we find
When we're making up reasons to shut off our minds.
I did find my notepad (eventually)
But by then it had drawn a new poem from me.

Graham Smith

Haiku

majestic aether
wheeling the stars and planets
through their perfect rounds

Don Kingfisher Campbell

Analogy Planet

Clouds race like dogs over land

There's a pot of steamy nimbus being cooked
rising from a hot pool surrounded by snow

Geyser springs are beautiful open sores

Undersea thermal bubbles endless cotton candy

Fire and water give birth to crusty daughter

Like a star being born in steam

Liquid rock cools hardens like chocolate shell

Is a volcano simply a giant pimple

When it blows there goes fiery pus

Boiling lava might as well be lighted ice cream

Millions of trees get knocked over like pick-up sticks

Volcano blown, now the scab is much smaller

Volcano dead not unlike stone sculpture

Mountainous fingers feel their way across earth
without moving more than inches a year

Big ants run get squashed by falling buildings

Earthquake fault merely seams on a baseball

Maybe a waterfall is just a runny nose

Carrie McKay

The Detective is In

Epideral - "The world is full of obvious things which nobody by any chance ever observes."
Sherlock Holmes Quote
-*The Hound of the Baskervilles*

Snoopy followed the cookie thief.
The brim of his hat focusing his vision,
he crept across the grassy yard
peering through his magnifying glass.
Each crumb flavored his sight
with anger not even sugar could coat.

His cloak flowing behind like a shadow,
he flattened at any sound and
slithered through brush like a snake.
His fierce gaze read the smallest print.
The left foot is smaller, his stride short
An industrial accident he deduced.

He followed the culprit clue by clue
straight to his base, the tallest ant hill.
He smiled grimly, blowing a single bubble
from his carefully placed pipe.
and hung the mandibled face drawing
next to the other Wanted Posters.

Rick Lupert

Ants

Today at lunch I was God.
The hungry masses gathered around me.
I rained bread from their sky.
It was French bread
No manna from this deity
I am a gourmet God
The crumbs of my lunch fed thousands
They were brought as offerings to the queen
They sculpted busts of me out of the larger pieces
They constructed temples in my honor out of hollowed out crusts
I was only there for a half hour
I won't return tomorrow
I may never
I will become part of their mythology
Holy wars will be fought in my name
Not that they know my name
They will call me food
And someday, they will eat me.

Shelby Hayes

Insanely Bloodthirsty

How did I become so insanely bloodthirsty, you ask? Oh, I don't know. I don't suppose watching YOUR beloved mentor get a stake in the heart and the beheaded would harm your mind, oh no... Of course it would! [giggle] And yes, I realize it was 10 years ago, but what are years to the undead?

I was very poor when I was turned. I was on the verge of death: death by starvation, death by thirst, death by disease. So diseased my *caring, loving* family tossed me on the corpse cart without a look back, without a tear shed; thrown into a giant grave with thirty other mortals and one vampire - my Sire. He was there because he wanted to feast on the newly dead.

As fate would have it, he began with me. I was so weak I didn't notice that he was sucking me dry until I had less than an ounce of life left. Then my Sire stopped, looked at me, shed a single bloody tear, and brought me to unlife. It seemed he'd always wanted a daughter.

But still, I haven't explained why I am so insanely bloodthirsty. My apologies, let me go on...

My Sire learnt me in the ways of the undead. He taught me for years and during that time, I was bonded to him. Why, he was my god (ouch!) and you... You killed him! Killed him just because you felt like it! Put a stake through his heart and an ax through his neck!

You took my Sire, my Go-... Lord! Because of you I went back on the streets. Who would have a 12-year-old bloodsucker for a daughter, hmm? I ate the poor, the homeless, and --- oh, pigeons.

That is why I am so insanely bloodthirsty; that is why I ate your tasty children; and that is why I am really going to enjoy eating you!

Steve Ramirez

The Zombie Cheesecake

At first, you didn't believe it:
the torn milk carton, dairy bleeding
down the refrigerator door.

How could you? Even when you found the torn remains
of this week's whole wheat loaf, and what can only
be described as a massacre of yogurt;
bits of Harvest Peach, Pina Colada and Mango Burst
extruded from their containers, like a cow turned inside out.

The one you'll kick yourself about,
the part in the horror movie where everybody
groans at your stupidity, was last night's leftover
casserole. It looked like it had leapt
from the bake ware dish, fell forty stories
and landed on the sidewalk of your Frigidaire.

You'd never think something like this could happen
to you, or the cheesecake you brought home last week,
like the other every day betrayals we ignore:

the phone calls from unknown numbers
that hang up at the sound of your voice,
how it gets harder to take the stairs every year,
or the bump on the back of your neck,
which you'll get checked out if it doesn't go away
in a week (or a month), and how you're going to get
your life in order, if you can just get through today.

Everything will be different tomorrow

Michael Cantin

Morning Tutelage with Alestair

The kitchen counter was uncharacteristically sparse
The oven, black and ponderous, sat, yawning:
Its' cryptic gaping maw awaiting an offering
as might an obscene alien deity.
And yet the stove top was the greater of oddities;
Its' five burners arranged into a blasphemous sigil

Mr. Crowley bade me to beat six eggs reverently.
Thrice and thrice again!
in a sacrificial silver bowl
He intoned that he would take to mortar and pestle
so as to fashion a savory rub.

Next the Master grimaced a command
to add virgin milk and chorizo sausage
(Purity and decadence in equal measure)
Then he, most surreptitious and unseen,
did add the final unnamed
(nee! Unnamable!)
ingredients to mine

Combined thus, the bowl's contents were reborn
and offered up to our hungering Iron God!

As shadows loomed malevolent,
candles lit themselves....
All the better for us to focus on our new task:
the gentle massaging of succulent and innocent bacon!
Then, our knives and wills in unison,
did we cleave it apart into long fleshy strips
Eerie blue flames of no discernible origin
cooked away the fat
atop the wrought sigil burners.

And then…..
true terror halted the pounding muscle
Nestled betwixt my aching ribs
With my voice tremulous and soft as mouse I spoke:
"Mr. Crowley," Said I
"May I be so bold?"
At this he nodded in ascension,
though his eyes did seem to search distant undreamt shores
"Scrambled eggs." I swallowed fearful, "are best served with cheese."
'Oh, insufferable Fates!" He lamented at the transgression
"I had forgotten"

And this is why
Hidden as lemuric worms may
in our sepulcher
of a breakfast nook
….our repast went
…………ungarnished

Seth Halbeisen

Vaya con Queso

(Go with cheese...)

Wonderful,
glorious,
    divine cheese.
Cheese, cheese,
  Cheesy,
    cheese.
Could there be anything better?
Well... Perhaps,
but you really shouldn't buy that.
Not really...
You can,
it's your funeral,
but it's never as satisfying.
Trust me...
I know.
But then there is cheese!
The truest,
most perfect dairy.
Swiss, Brie,
and my personal favorite,
Cheddar!
So admired and revered,
its slang for money!
"Do you have any extra cheddar?"
Wondrous Cheese.
Expertly solidified,
carefully aged and jam packed with happiness.
Creamy and dreamy,
extruded or shaped.
My dreams are filled with slices,
wedges and great wheels of glorious cheese!
Inundated with Cholesterol,

my heart flutters,
    drowning in a prolonged,
        tangy cardiac arrest.

Rick Lupert

Sandwich

I ordered a sandwich at the coffee shop
An hour went by and I still hadn't received it yet.
My stomach rumbled as if to remind me.
I asked the counter man about it and he assured me that
      he hadn't forgotten.
The bread was still in the oven,

Two days Passed.

I was becoming quite hungry.
The counter man admitted that it might have slipped his mind.
"What had slipped his mind" I asked.
"The sandwich you ordered" he answered.
It had slipped my mind too.
We agreed that I should get the sandwich soon.
There was such a resolution to our agreement that we didn't
think about it again for a week.
By this time I was famished.

It was the stomach pains which caused me to say
      to the counterman

"Say, what about that sandwich."
He said "Oh yeah, your sandwich.
I'll put three of my best people on it."

And so he did,

and six days later,
the sandwich was delivered to my table.
Apparently it had been ready for a day and a half,
but some things had come up that they needed to take care of.
They apologized for the delay,

and gave me a free Diet-Coke for my patience.

By this time,
my body was so horribly emaciated,
that the coke flowed down the new craters in my skin,
like Niagara Falls just met the Grand Canyon
at the screening of a new artsy film.

This was my Doug Knott Metaphor.

I requested that the sandwich be liquefied,
and then fed to me intravenously.

Three weeks later,
They complied with this request.
But by this time
I had permanent brain damage,
scurvy,
and had lost the use of my legs and arms.

Needless to say this was reflected in their tip.

I dictated a letter to the management.
People were scolded,
New policies were developed.
It is good to be a consumer activist

Lauren

Pedro: The Taco Stylist

Pedro is a taco and a hair dresser.
He is the best hair dresser in the fast food company.
He uses special hair products, like
salsa shampoo, *guacamole* conditioner, and a *sour cream* rinse.
He's got just the right mixture of spices to attract the lady foods.
Then there was a problem.
Pedro chose the hairstyles for the foods, but the foods didn't like that.
"*Lettuce* choose the styles! Your styles are *cheesy!*" said the foods.
Pedro agreed the foods should have their choice of styles.
Afterwards, everything returned to normal, and
his *menu* of customers *grew* full again!

Leanne Hunt

The Unicyclists' Union Votes are In

Juggling is optional, but we got the fire permit. Flaming
puck unicycle hockey, catch if you can. Unicon
here we come, every other year. It's biennial.
We feel the road, and wheel size can
increase speed. Movement is the key. Pedal
to balance. We fall and we correct, point and counterpoint,
to maintain stability. With no gears, no brakes, we stand
alone. We freestyle our aesthetics, grind our tricks, and race
uphill and down. Look, ma, no hands.
Our team sports are all individual competitions.

Raundi K. Moore-Kondo

I Am a Parrot in a Cage

I try to keep the place clean.
I try to make it look as if I haven't been here at all.
I dream there is someone knocking and trying to break in.
I am only a broken record.
I can't do anything to keep a stranger out.
All I ask for is a lock that I can depend on.

I understand that the world is vast.
Probably more than a million newspapers wide.
I could see as many of them as I want.
If only I could bring myself to fly.

I am a screaming mime whose cage will not stay shut.
I cry over little things like busted latches.
and crumbs—

When there is no one around for me to mimic.
I touch the bars to be sure they are solid.
I kick the empty dish.
Nothing remains but dust.
I pretend there is a hawk in the eucalyptus tree outside the window--
waiting.
I feel safe knowing I am in here and he is out there.
I am Technicolor winged beast afraid of the black shadows I make.

I want to be chased from this place—
driven out into the night and shooed away.
I see the black holes in the eyes of owls that suck in the night.
I hear sparrows squawking to survive.
Crows cavorting and complaining.
Their sounds of panic have never meant anything to me.
I do not even speak my own language.

Sometimes I wonder why I have never breached these bars.

Then I wonder why anyone would--
but, I've never felt the wind.

RD Armstrong

What Unites Us

The need to feel like
You are a human being
Is universal
Whether you are trying
To make ends meet
In Baghdad
Tehran
Haifa
Basra
Tripoli
Paris
Belfast
Detroit
South Central
Birmingham
West Oakland
Riverside
Or even Long Beach

That is what unites us
This longing to be treated
As if our lives matter

Graham Smith

Haiku

rooted in earth and
stone, drinking light and water
branching to the sky

Matt Foster

Tall

A tree standing tall
watching over the city
providing protection

Illumines sun
providing its light to us
So warm and perfect

People in the street
Working, eating, or driving
Living out the day

The wondrous birds,
Not caring about a lot
Flying here and there

Leslie Maryann Neal

The Apple Never Falls Far from the Tree-- She Jumps

She isn't the apple of her father's knotted eye.
Pointing with a twig at her brown spot,
her crooked stem, he reminds her
that one bad apple spoils the barrel.

Her sisters are forbidding fruit,
always flaunting their red, delicious curves.
Her father praises their clear skin.

She once thought he would grow
to love her, too, if she ripened.
But no amount of sun or shadow
would flush her yellow cheek.

So she twists her stem free
and lands in a bristle of grass.
The orchard keeper rustles toward her,
a basket under his flannel-sleeved arm.
Pointing her one pale leaf out like a flag,
she sits up straight and tries to blush.

Alexis Tan

The Fall That Never Came

I waited for fall, but fall never came
Nobody seemed to remember.
The pumpkins never grew,
It was as hot as ever!
Leaves stuck and stayed green
No one sold Halloween costumes
The calendar clearly said October.
The turkeys were never roasted,
But grew fat in days to come.
Now the calendar said December
But winter never came.
The snow didn't fall,
The conifers stayed the same.
Me always waiting,
For the winter snow to fall.
Now spring is next,
For March was still to come,
But why in the world could it be still summer?

Anahita Amirshahi

The Anticipation of Winter

My face pressed against
The cool glass of the window,
I breathe,
And my steaming breath blurs
Trees with bare branches
No green grass
The world is dead
With me living in this
Barren wasteland.
Waiting, watching
For a sign of life.
Other than me and my
Silent, sleeping
Dreaming dog.
Wrapped in
A soft, warm blanket,
My hearth roaring
With blazing hot fire,
I anticipate
The first snowflake.
Suddenly what I see
Outside of my
Frosty window
Opens my heart
To feel better love.
Down falls the first
Snowy white flake of winter.
Twirling and twisting
Like a ballerina.
Followed by many more just like it.
Followed by my satisfaction.

Vanessa

Gingerbread House

For Christmas they constructed a gingerbread house.
Not a little house that you break apart with your hands
and chomp on as you sit in front of the fireplace

The sort of house that you saunter into and sit by the icing-laced
fireplace they keep roaring inside

I walked up to it, white with frosting and dusted in sparkling
sugar with whimsicle designs decorating the door

I fumbled with the frosting door and its fluffy marshmallow
over peanut brittle knob to find the infernal thing locked

And suddenly the early Christmas present they presented
to me and specifically instructed that I not taste suddenly made some
sense

Out of my pocket I picked a carefully carved candy cane
who's peculiarly carved tip twinkled in the Christmas lights

The cane came in contact with a chocolate keyhole
and the sugar white door and its sweet handle swung open with ease

To say the inside made outside look simple would simply be an
understatement
Tiles of gingerbread and tastefully colored taffy created a checked floor

It was a game to get where you wanted to go without getting gummed
up
and glued down by stupidly stepping on a taffy tile

Who's idea where the taffy tiles anyway?
The taffy tiles and toffee tables and tinsel lined window.

Well, the windows were nice but whatever else seemed stuck
in taffy and toffee and too much cinnamon

Cinnamon everywhere. Cinnamon on the cookies
on the toffee table. Cinnamon sprinkled
on the perfectly prettified pine tree picked out by much too perky
crafters

Sugar and snow, and sugar cookies decorated
the fartherest wall sitting sparkle in the corner.

Ornaments settled in shining white snow and sugar cookies
sparkling with several tiny granules

And red. Everywhere red. Every rueful corner riddled with red.
Red candies, and bulbs, and Christmas lights, and red sugar,
and red-nosed reindeer, and ridiculous red santa hats

The couch is crafted of marshmallow and covered in red tinsel.
How in heck do they get comfortable on that thing?

And two busy-body builders, this candy house's crafters cuddle
in the corner with their scalding hot chocolate laughing and blushing
red with the heat from a fancy cookie fueled fire

Lena

Spring

Spring falls off
little brown branches.
The wind
blows spring off course.

Noor Bashir

My Seasons

Spring, spring is when flowers blossom up from the ground
While bees and butterflies enjoy the sounds

Summer, summer is when fireflies fill the midnight air
While I sit in my hammock and stare

Fall, fall is when leaves flutter to the ground
A rainbow of red, yellow and golden brown

Winter, winter is when peaceful showers of snow cover the earth
While animals snuggle in their hearth.

Eric Lawson

When the Cows Come Home

When the cows come home, our goose is cooked.
Do you have any idea what they'll do to us?
Have you ever seen an ill-tempered herd?
It's not pretty even in an ice cream ad way.
When the cows come home, we can't hide anymore.
They'll know what we've done and we have to answer to them.
All of them!
At once!
And no, they won't accept half-hearted moos.
When the cows come home, we'll have to clean everything!
Clean their houses, their cars, their coffee shops galore.
Oh, and they are cruel task masters those cows.
No milking it on the chores this time.
When the cows come home, the party will be over.
The music will have to be turned off or banned forever.
No more dancing or hopping or tapping along.
They're worse than the parents in Footloose.
It doesn't matter what you say.
The cows have heard it all before.
It doesn't matter if you were only tagging along.
The cows will still udderly despise you.
It doesn't matter what your background is.
Be you rich, poor, tall, skinny, fat, short.
The cows will curdle us all together.
It's curtains for all of us to be certain.
When the cows come home, I don't want to be here.
They will arrive in suped-up go-karts from Hawaii.
Today's cows drive go-karts that can hydroplane.
They will come and make us into cute dairy products.
We're sorry, cows! We didn't know you'd be home...ever.
We take it all back, cows! Every blurted bovine punch line.
Please show mercy on the wicked humans, great cows!
Our only flaw is that we exceed when it comes to excess.
Next time, if there is indeed a next time, we promise you:

We will send you on an even slower boat to China,
a more dangerous treasure hunt with no maps,
and tea time waltzes in the Sahara sans sunblock,
if you will, in turn, promise us puny humans,
to pretty, pretty please with sprinkles on top,
call us first to let us know you're on the way, hmm?
Who do you think pays for all your lavish vacations?
You ungrateful, self-absorbed, four-legged cheese sticks!

G. Murray Thomas

Cows On The Freeway

Cows spilled all over the freeway
    by another amusing anecdote
    on the traffic report.
Cows standing, dazed,
the carcasses of their traveling companions
scattered around them
hinting at something,
    something they can't understand
    yet obviously important.
While more things they can't understand
zip by
too fast to catch
    or even focus on
yet, again, obviously important.
These cows know
    there is something they must do
    RIGHT NOW!!
But they sure don't know
what the hell it could be.

I can't tell you how often
I feel like a cow
on a freeway.

Alexis Tan

Rainbow Fish

A rainbow magical fish,
So precious, so beautiful,
But yet so dangerous,
Its wonderful swirls
Lure many a brave souls to their death.
She pushes them into a black hole,
Where they are stretched And pulled apart into spaghetti strands,
So yet, she is unknown…

Darian Agredano

Nibble... Nibble...   CHOMP!!!

Mankind has always had a fear of deep water and what lives beneath. Just imagine you are in the Tropics, relaxing in a natural spring leading off a river. You are all alone. You can't really touch the bottom, but that doesn't bother you. It's so peaceful. You feel a nibble on your toe, but that doesn't bother you. Your whole body is tingling, but you just shrug it off. Ouch! That hurt. You pull your foot to your face and examine it. There is a small circular bite mark. Blood trickles from it. You begin to feel uneasy. "Ouch, ouch, ouch, damnit!" More biting! You begin to panic. Your mind is telling you, "Get out! Get out!" You try to grasp the rock walls but the water and heat has made them moist and slippery, and you can't seem to pull yourself out. Ahh! Something bit your toe badly. You call for help, but there is no one around. You had requested to take this hike to the springs alone. You had argued with your wife and son. The searing pain all around you is overwhelming. It's harder and harder to stay above the water. You search for the rope ladder to climb out. There it is, but you are in too much pain. Fumbling with the rope, you get up three steps, but then lose your balance and fall back in. You are sinking deeper and deeper. The sun glistens through the water above you. Almost completely numb, everything seems to be getting darker, and redder. Becoming wrapped, consumed, enveloped by darkness. A last thought crosses your mind, "didn't put on any sun block."

Lena

Shells

Shells sing when you are not listening,
their songs fly above the waves,
twisting notes into music

Leslie Maryann Neal

Mermaid

When I was a child, I could breathe underwater.
I never told anyone about this strange ability,
these imagined gills. I was a secret mermaid
walking land, my tail and fins unnoticed.

Now I plunge into the deep end and fear
devours me with the water. I come to the surface
coughing, panicked at the space beneath my feet.
The dark sky doesn't end with the land.
I am treading water in it; the ten feet around me
is infinite space. I am suspended like a satellite,
light glinting off my surfaces. My eyes stinging,
I watch my t-shirt flow in the zero gravity.
I am breathing only air, pushing through water
with only arms and legs; my fins are gone.
I'm just a girl with amphibian memories.
I am trying to swim.

Andy Buell

Fish Tank Diver

The life of a plastic fish tank diver
is stationary and boring.
He stands guard over a treasure chest
filled with fool's gold and bubbles.

His gaze is fixed,
focused on point beyond the glass.
That was where he saw her
leaning close to the glass to feed the fish.

She was an air breather,
a dry-land girl.
She was beautiful,
give up your treasure and learn to dry out beautiful,
hold your breath to keep from scaring her away beautiful,
wish you could jump start your plastic guts and run away with her
beautiful,
compelled to tell her nothing but the truth beautiful.

Since Welsh is the only language
that can be spoken under water
he confessed with it:
"wrth eu bodd"
"fy nghariad yn unig"

As his oxygenation broke the surface
she turned and leaned into his gaze
tapping the glass to say hello.
It was the first time
he'd felt the click clack of
his plastic heartbeat.

Anahita Amirshahi

Jerome

The boy was bored in class,
His mind a blank slate.
"What to do next?" he
Started to debate.

Deciding on graffiti,
He pulled out a pencil
And on the bare desk,
He began to stencil.

A warrior formed under his hand;
Instead of legs, he had a pole
And an amputated arm-
This sketch was not a whole.

The class came to an end,
And the boy went home.
But the soldier stayed, and
Called himself Jerome.

Next morning came,
And girls sat at Jerome's table.
They didn't see him at first,
And then they were able.

The girls gave him hair,
And a screw for a hand.
They made it so he was
Standing on grassy land.

They too left him,
Again he was lone.
The sun had gone down
It no longer shone.

Jerome was by himself
All through the night.
Then he was accompanied again,
Come morning light.

A cleaning man came,
With damp rag and mop.
Prepared to clean
Every tabletop.

With his cart of dusty water
And his bottle of cleaning stuff,
The tired man wiped Jerome's life away
Not thoroughly, but enough.

Jerome died a brave soldier,
His head and torso a puddle.
The pole of his legs
Had become a muddle.

When the boy came back
To see the product of a bore,
He saw that his beloved
Jerome was no more.

Maggie G. Brown

Shape Shifter

Blue timid eyes,
searching for something

Peach lips moving to the song
of the wind

A dress curling out,
shading the cloudy sky
with a red tone

Brunette hair,
waving along in thin air

Black boots hard against
the soft slithering grass

A touch of lightning
to play with the sound of thunder

Rain,
tip tap
on the ground singing a rhythmic song

She is alone in a meadow,
alone with herself,
though her body may not show,
she is everything

She's a bird, a lion, a wolf,
willing and strong
to start a new life
in a small place

She is a dragonfly,

hiding from the storm

She is a fish,
swimming in the clouds

She is a star shining,
and a little speck of dust,
just below the one tree that stands
on its own

She is that tree,
that rain drop,
each molecule,
and each plant and anthill

She is a mother to nature,
that little area in the wilderness

mysterious,
home.

Andy Buell

A Bored Ghost

The hollow in my chest cavity
is a pack of bored ghosts.
They've been haunting here for ages
scaring anyone trying
to come inside just for laughs.
Chasing anyone away before they have
a chance to make a home there.

I don't know when they got here,
but they are photodermatitis pale
and have forgotten the taste
of fresh air in their lungs.
I know they were still pumping blood
through their veins when
I first welcomed them in.

Even though they
outstayed their welcome
long before they gave up living,
I've always been too polite
to ask any of them to leave.

They've started planning
new scare tactics for when
their Boo's no longer work.
I'm crossing my fingers
the next visitor has bravery to spare.

Cynthia Quevedo

Bluebeard Wears Tommy Bahama

There's a man in my basement.

He has gray curly hair.

He wears a Tommy Bahama shirt.

I shout, "Shoo, go away!"
like I'm shooing a scrawny stray cat.

He scuffles into the dark recesses.

I only go down there
when I need something;
the stairs are broken and worn.

Who is he? What's he doing there?

I only ask these questions
when I'm safe up the stairs.

Ken Schmidt

My Shadow

I thought about my shadow today. It started because a poet mentioned that her shadow was already embracing the shadow of the man that she was about to meet.

That made me think. I remember seeing my shadow yesterday, but today, I don't know. I remember that it was sunny. I don't remember seeing my shadow all day. Did it go somewhere? If so, where did it go? Is it taking care of me, or is it up to trickery? It could be up to trickery. You know, shadows are sneaky things. They will stretch out along the path for a while and then just JUMP up on a wall. Only to DART into a doorway and then POW back on the wall. They will be close to you during the day but come evening you can tell that they are trying to get away. They start stretching out from you. Farther and farther. Then at the moment of sunset, POOF, where did they go? Did they go to a shadow place? I am sure that they are all together, wherever . . . . shadows . . . . go.

Now the question is, what are they up to? Are they planning tomorrow's escapades? Remember, we do not know if they are friends or foes. Foes stuck to us for half of their existence. They may be mad at us for this. But it's not my fault. I never even thought about it. Oohhhh, that could be it. The shadows are unhappy because we don't think about them enough. How would you like to be ignored most of the time? How would you feel if your shadow didn't even know if you were there today?

I remember one time, I was in the park, and a pretty lady was sitting on a park bench. Well her shadow's butt was sticking out between the back and the bottom of the bench that she was sitting on. I was being a devil that day, so I made my shadow reach up and try to pinch the lady's butt. But I think my shadow yelled out to her shadow, Run, Run, he's making me pinch you. And I think her shadow told the pretty lady because just as I was about to make my shadow pinch her, she got up and left. It must be that her shadow told her. Well, neither me or my shadow got into trouble that day. I think that our shadows sometimes look out for us.

Now, back to what they are doing tonight.

I wonder if my shadow has just met the love of my life,

and will tell me,

tomorrow.

Ralph R. Moore

Suwannee

When I was a boy my grandparents had a 160 acre farm in the backwoods of the northern Florida county of Suwannee that was said to be 15 miles from the river. At times they would make the trek to the river for a "fish-fry." My family lived further south in Hillsborough county and visits to the grandparent's farm were rare and special.

When I was around 4 years old I was left there with them, without knowing why and not caring. In later years it came to me it was about the time a younger brother was born and the parents wanted to get me out of the way. While I was at the getaway farm the grandparents, along with some of the local relatives decided to go to the river for a fish-fry, and since I had never been before, this was an exciting time for me.

Grandpa never used horses for the farm work, saying they didn't have the stamina of mules, so he hitched up one of them to the buggy and we made the trip to the river. That evening they built a fire on the riverbank, and we had a fresh-caught fish dinner, although at that time and place it was called supper. Being a natural water-child, in this beautiful setting, with the river flowing smoothly between trees covered with the hanging moss, and growing right to the banks, it was an experience I could never forget.

In later years thoughts of that river and experience would return to me many times, and after going to school and learning Stephen Foster's song I was eventually inspired to "make-up" a river song myself. I say make-up because I was, and still am, musically illiterate and couldn't write the song, but could by trial and error, form the words and the tune.

Finally, in 1951 I did just that, but in the 62 years since then the words, themselves, have never been written down, but have been kept alive, squirming around in my head and looking for a place to settle. So here it is, and I can see now there are some errors in it, but decided to leave it as is. I've lived with it all these years, and good or bad, I'm in no mood to change it now.

Ralph R. Moore

Suwannee

My Childhood sweetheart is a beautiful thing,
She flows through the land that I love.
I look through the trees on the edge of
Her banks and see the starlight above.

O beautiful Suwannee keep rolling along,
You'll still be here when I'm gone
But I'll love you forever, and that's a
Long time, O childhood sweetheart of mine.

I remember the times in days long gone by
I sat on my grand daddy's knee
In a pine board house he told me strange tales,
They were of Suwannee, you see.

O beautiful Suwannee keep rolling along,
You'll still be here when I'm gone.
But I'll love you forever, and that's a
Long time, O childhood sweetheart of mine.

I've been the world over, I've seen all the sights,
But your beauty is still unsurpassed
I've come back to you and I'm here
now to stay, contented forever at last.

O beautiful Suwannee keep rolling along
You'll still be here when I'm gone.
But I'll love you forever, and that's a
Long time, O childhood sweetheart of mine.

Annelise Cramm

Laughs

Chuckles, giggles,
Chortles, guffaws
Tittering, too
Laughs of every kind
All of these come from
The room of happiness
Inside
You

Karina Cramm

Ode To Rotten Banana Peel

A greasy black banana peel,
Lying forgotten in the clutter,
It smells deliciously like the gutter,
I lick my lips at the thought of the fruit it once held,
I wish I hadn't eaten it last Christmas!

JL Martindale

Fountain of My Youth

Despite eternal drought, I turn the spigot
let him run through sprinkles in Superman Underoos
like I did when I was his age.

I suppose I should feel oppressive guilt
hovering like the sweltering August heat
But I don't.
I let the water run, and run, and run
so we can chase rainbows through waterfalls
and squish black mud between pale naked toes.

Annelise Cramm

Nighttime

Darkness everywhere,
An owl hoots
Crickets chirp
SUDDENLY
Children run into the clearing
Laughing happily,
Playing flashlight tag

Vanessa

Fairy Doll

Poor broken fairy doll
Sitting slumped against the wall
Missing left arm and right eye
Left one color of the sky
Shining sheer wings ripped right off
Somewhere far off they've been tossed
A sparkling skirt nearly ripped to shreds
And the sparkle in a left-behind eye dead
Poor broken fairy doll
Sitting slumped against the wall
I look at you and hope and pray
That you'll be put back together some day

Kelsey Bryan Zwick

jacaranda song

down the street at Jackie's, in her yard
we play dolls, purple in the tea cups
sipping petals inside her playhouse, sweet stick
on the tongue, I keep eyeing the dogs
Jackie's dogs, they are huge, and pacing outside
the plastic window, bodies bigger than the frame

they are all jaws and sharp teeth
the terror of raptor clash claws
their muscled breathing, fills my belly
the dogs, they are looking at me
pushing the little red door open
someone has filled my ankles
with stones, running against
the weight of myself
and the dogs, they chase me
they'll rip me like a possum
carry me bloody like a rat

Jackie's yard ends, I can't stop running
scrape against the pavement
and those dogs, larger than before
are on top of me
I need them to bite me
scratch me from my sparkle tank
my place is quiet, mommies
at the hospital, alabaster

the room where everyone is small
getting radiated behind a lead wall
so sick, not even the nurses

can touch her, I cannot feel my body
the baby is skinny, on formula
my brother sings in his sleep
mommy has a bump in her boobie
bump in her boobie, I do not hear
dad's been crying at the bar

and the dogs won't bite
won't chew up my bones
only lick my skinned knees
sitting there, on the patio
waiting for a band aid
all I can see is their sharp teeth
they are daggers, spiked
bloody with my blood

Darian Agredano

The park

The park is an interesting phenomenon in itself. With a wide range of people, various plant life, and a strange assortment of small creatures. It's a hand full of ecosystems mushed together. With trees lining the barriers, and giant clumps of iron and plastic, which bring children joy. Small children playing tag, and middle-aged adults jogging, inertly wishing that they could join the children in there antics. Wailing toddlers, screaming for candy to distract their parents while their friends sneak up from behind, and steal the entire box. In a park, all reason and common sense is forgotten. All the trees are climbable. All the insects are edible. All the fountains are swimable. The parents huddle together, sobbing, realizing that they should have just gotten a dog. A familiar song pierces the wall of noise, a familiar jingle associated with sugar. There is dead silence as the jingle continues. Then, there's an explosion. The race is on. Dogs thrown, the elderly shoved to the ground, all in an effort to get to the ice cream mans truck first. The sugar rush has set in and the sticky children continue making more noise than ever, dropping their cones in the sand, smearing the melted remains of their treats all over there faces. But, the parents will soon be able to relax for as Newton's Law says, "what comes up, must come down." Hours and hours later heaps of unconscious children lay everywhere, slumped over the swings, hanging out of trash cans, and strewn about the tennis courts. They are carried out by the truckload and loaded into strollers, or simply dragged by the ankles. Then they are shoved into car seats, and driven home. Other than a few gray hairs, the parents aren't worse for wear. But there eye twitches knowing the process will be repeated tomorrow.

Ruth Blue

Robot Robot

Robot Robot made of steel
the new yet rustic feel
glorious glamorous teal.
Someday doomed to take over
never to learn the truth
until it's all over.

Steve Ramirez

Before We Knew It Was Episode IV

My brother is a genius.
He always knew Han was cooler than Luke.

I didn't care, because dad's cheap metal
flashlight kinda looked like a lightsaber.

It was the year we started having Christmas
at Uncle Ben's house. The place with posters
of bullfights from some place we'd never been.

A place they called Mexico.

We got to sleep over, sleeping bags spread across
deep shag. Christmas Eve was the perfect night
for ghost stories while cars tiptoed past,
their tires slick with rain. Christmas Day
we planned to open the shiny blue box
hidden beneath their bed.

Dungeons & Dragons.

It was a good year in our house.

Uncle Ben and Aunt Mamie woke us with their laughter
when they tried to hide the presents under the tree.

They hadn't expected to find Han and Luke
protecting baby Jesus in the manger,
or to see stormtroopers trying to blast their way
past the ceramic camels and Three Wise Men.

The children in our family learned early
to stand guard at night.

Karina Cramm

My Room

Messy dresser, messy room
In my closet a large raccoon
Dirty socks here and there
Under the bed there is full of hair
In the bookshelf monkeys hang
Behind the dresser is an orangutan
Notebook paper under the mattress,
So I can write, write, write

Ben Trigg

Hiding

When you absolutely must hide from your mother at Sears,
go for a circular rack of coats.
Their heavy material will block both light
and her frantic cries as she struggles to find you.
Your impromptu fort of winter wear will give you
the space you've been needing to dream.
There are no chores to distract
from the wars in your head,
no homework making demands.
When your playtime is over remember to put on a convincing show.
You must wail and cry, plead terror.
You have chosen to arouse either sympathy or wrath.
The sincerity of your lie is the roll of the dice.

Heather Autumn Love

Why, As a Child, I Hated Taking Grandma to the Bus Depot *

Because that's where the crazy people were.

Like mannequins, they stood
before the maps and restrooms
Their bedraggled manes dangled;
their faces, the coldest symphony of soot.

They hummed and whispered.
Skinny arms flapped at invisible insects.
Their glassy eyes locked upon things unseen.

I clung to my mother's hand.
But there, she was not the mother I knew:

not the mother who shrieked me indoors
whenever someone neared the fence;
not the mother who pounded deep into my mind
that danger was waiting to swallow me whole.

At the bus depot,
she chatted idly to my grandmother.
She was blind to the terrifying zoo about us.
She did not sense how I stood frozen as steel,
or how everything within me quaked.

So, I shut down
and counted the minutes,
praying myself invisible.

I was so eager for the bus to tug Grandma from the sidewalk,
and said my goodbyes too quickly.

The car ride home was silent.

There was no teaching moment,
no scolding or explanation,
no foreshadowing of the bitter genetic lottery
waiting to flood my veins with nickels.

This was years before my mind began to implode.

This was years before my skull weighted with stones,
and pressed so heavy against my chest;

before I found myself staring
from the other side of the glass,
my limbs petrified wood, unmoving.

And my mother said nothing.

I still see them everywhere.
The ghosts of the bus depot:
those shattered souls I once thought demons.

I find them lingering lonely on benches,
and wandering cracked sidewalks.
They hold up their broken mirror,
and sing me a tune I learned too well.

Each time, my heart pulses against my ribs,
and aching atonement fills my bones.
Each time, from deep in the marrow I hear:

but, for the grace of God

* apologies to Cecilia Wolloch who inspired this title.

Peggy Dobreer

Somniloquy,
by which I Mean Parasomnia

>too sand the surface of my sigh
is only this the creaking walk of
he I going gone to stay again and
force be true to rock and peel
like thunder cloud be giving husk
to plant this oven burns hot clean
and fast we bake the bread we roast
the corn we sky the limit off

Jaimes Palacio

Burning Down The Stars

You sat on my carpet in the middle of
the floor. There were others
there, in my room. Two of them dating
already. We were both third wheels. You weren't doing

much. Just sitting cross-legged, playing
with some over-sized glasses. Not really flirting. You had someone
waiting for you later. We were both young. But you...
more dangerously so. In this pause, I think we became

friends. This unbearably beautiful
intermission scaffolding such wild
possibility; momentum of a new history careening
dangerously like a drunk driving tank.

How fleeting this feeling, this movement
of the heart pumping madly with impossible hope. This is
what the stupid guide books tell us is love. Part voodoo
chemistry and part slight of hand. We are all

magicians when we are in love. We crave the lightning
in our blood. Call it magic. In this way, we make illusions
palpable. In this way, we bastard our vision with the
non-existent.

But this is not a lecture. Nor is it a love
story. We came close. Tumbling like Babylon through
my door giddy silly with laughter: not drunk, but just unchained
enough...We came close. Riding shotgun in my car. Letting me know
that if I ever got engaged, you planned to disrupt the wedding. We
came

close. You kissed me once... But it was just to shut
my big mouth up. If we were honest, maybe you would admit

that you had loved me. In that small galaxy of time. Before
the spaceship of our trajectory lost it's guidance system

and crashed screaming, burning the stars down. Turning the sky
biblical. The screeching, lonely cry of birds losing to gravity.
If we were honest than maybe I would admit I was too much wrong
for anything but accidents.

You are there.
I am here.
I am not missed.
The years have made me...
air. The darkness calling me
home.

Lydia Quevedo

Softly Through the Night

She walks
softly in the dark,
her foot on nothing but
still stepping,
still shining with a light
that envelops her whole body,
that is nothing save
the intensity of her soulfire, the
light of her love that still burns even though
he stopped loving her,
stopped seeing
her,
long ago.
But she didn't stop
seeing him.
She didn't stop
seeing anyone,
but then they stopped seeing her,
until the fire of her soul told her like a crystal ball
to step into this world of darkness
because
nothing mattered,
nothing but
him.
Now she stopped
seeing everyone, and
everyone stopped
seeing her, and
she walked slowly through
the darkness,
shining foot stepping
on nothing but still feeling,
still stepping,

part of the only light
in this place.
And she walked,
looking for the only other person
that she could see,
he,
who stood in both worlds
simultaneously.
Whenever she found him she would
step in front of him and stare
hungrily,
like echo at Narcissus,
having learned long ago that she could not speak
to him, and
could not touch him,
whence her fingers would cause him to
disappear. She
would then have to wander,
wearily, until she
found him again, so
she chose to see his face
over letting him vanish,
even if
his eyes stared through her indifferently,
even if he never responded to her words,
not even to her touch although
his image did vanish,
but she didn't care
because
what of this was different from that other world
that she had lived in,
once?
She wasn't part of his world,
he was all of hers,
and all she ever saw was him
anyway, so
the blackness never bothered her.
She didn't know
if she was in a new world entirely,

or stuck in her mind, gone mad
with heartbreak,
or if she walked through all things mistily,
walked through her world ghostly,
and although she was there only saw
him. She
stood in the nothingness and looked
and
saw a distantly glowing figure,
he,
like a ghost,
walking, talking, dancing,
but not with her, to her.
Her approach made no difference,
it didn't matter if she spoke or not,
but she placed her hands
in the air beside him
and waltzed with him
in painful pretend glory.
And all she saw was
him,
an all he saw was
nothing,
so what was different
from the world she was in before?
Suddenly in confusion
he paled, then
laughed nervously to his
real partner, said:
"For a moment you looked
like a girl I knew,
once,
but I
can't recall her name,
and now her face has vanished too.
Just as well."
Tears stung
her
face,

and his blurred like watercolors,
but she danced,
on and on,
refusing to stop,
but her trembling fingers,
her distracted eye,
combined to force one mistake
of the placement of her fingers,
which brought his face,
his waist,
in contact with
her hands, and he
paled, widened his eyes,
in shock, in alarm,
whispered,
"I felt her. I know it.
There's no mistaking it. It
was her,
though it couldn't be,
possibly…"
His
voice began to fade,
his glow to dim,
and she
was alone again, weeping
tears hot with anguish.
She
fell to her knees
on the floor unseen,
and released two painful sobs
from her tense, hot chest.
Tears,
glowing, fell, and vanished,
then their flow ceased,
quenched, and
she stood,
face calm, almost grim,
wild but determined.
And she walked softly in the night,
glowing feet treading

           on nothing
          yet treading
    as she went, seeing nothing,
          seeing no one,
           none save him.
     And what was different
     from the world she had
         inhabited before?

Cassy Agredano

To be a dancer

Jumping, leaping, rolling, dripping with sweat.
Having to learn step after step, before the big night.
Working up to goals people say are impossible.
Following a dream, whether or not made by them.
Each class brings a new thrill, not knowing what they'll learn.
Solos, learning, practice, everything is expected.
People underestimate them, but they really try.
They get yelled at, they hurt, but they keep going.
When the big night comes, the lights go dim.
When they come up again they give you a great show, no matter how they feel.
They go up there and do it.

Stefano Capobianco

Be (What You Dream)

In my dream,
There is a peace
A sense of life
Where we are free
The pain and tears
Lay in ashes behind me

By the road
There is sign
That says believe in who you are
But you can't see
At the speed you've been travelling

It is with passion
That courage finds its path
It is with kindness
That love find growth
With every effort there is a change

When I awake
I will smile with joy
And be thankful
I'm still alive
And in each moment
Live for what I have dreamed.

Maggie G. Brown

A World in a Dream

Eyes closed to find a place
where the mind met life

Days were as blue
as a spilled over can of sky

Its harmony pressed
against your ear drums
like butter to a bowl

Colors fixed upon
every loop, twirl and lace,
circled each other
then unraveled
out into the complexion
of the landscape

Life felt full of whimsy,
a light danced in the shadows,
crept up onto the walls
and managed to twist its way
to the light bulb that hung above an idea

It was such a favored place
that no one could discuss
over a book or table

All of dawn was still,
except one bird chirping
the awakening song
as the dreams of the night
took away and out of sight

That world would never be found,

when the day enveloped itself into its natural state,
where no one knew what transfixed their minds
the night before.

Raundi K. Moore-Kondo

Sweetest Dreams
for Ken Schmidt

Goodnight to the pitter-patter
of sleep-clumsy feet,
and to the giggles bubbling up the stairs.

Its time for bunny slippers, bath-time ducks,
and baby bunting zipper-ups.

Let's have a bedtime-story mountain climb,
make pillow-fluffing battle cries.
and sing lullabies composed on rocking horse
and Dobro steel.

Bring on the pudgy-armed squeezes
and the milk and honey-laced kisses.

Wallow in the yawns and cuddles.
Here come the sleepy snuggles.

Say a little prayer with me
and wish upon first stars.

Feed moon cheese to our Martian mice
and trace wooly sheep tracks
across the sheets.

All my angels watch over you.
The red-rooster waits on their command.
They keep the bedclothes tuckled up tight.
They quiet the yowls of milk-hungry midnight,
and soothe the snores of daylight-indifferent dogs.

They are ever watchful.
Taking turns with winks, blinks and nods.

Sprinkling dream dust,
caressing cool cheeks,
and Crayola-coloring your rooftop dreams.

Moonbeams spot light your secret night flights
and cotton candy laden your landing site.

A houseboat bobs outside the harbor.
You are safe and sound.

The crowned and rightful King of the desert castle
has returned.
Your stone minions stand at the ready.

Sleep can now rest easy.

Every joy I know is bundled up in you.
All there is for me to do,
is wait for you to rise and shine.

All I ask for are picture postcards
of your sweetest dreams.

Lori McGinn

Emma had a Monet dream

I heard today the older you get the less you dream
I started taking more vitamin b12 under the tongue
I started closing my inner ears
Wearing shades indoors

We are watching the water roll round the drain
It goes round and round
Like the song we always sing that is the same

The wheels on the bus go round and round
The wipers on the bus go swish, swish, swish
The animals on the bus go up and down
All over this town

Our morning glories used to climb up string webs
Custard tummies full bloom, dreaming
Cradling the Prussian blue sky

When I dreamed red fire was
A verb on my tongue
Green streams cleansed me
Like forgiveness
For the first time birds enter into her eyes

Living and breathing in watercolor worlds
Emma sleeps
Safe and warm
Baby blanket clutched in her small hand
In her land of ducks, geese and wild turkeys
Emma's eyes are big and the pond has no shore

Nhhhhhh

"To speak in one's sleep is to dance between worlds." -Piper Gandin

      Plock dee plock
            And soosssh soosssh
      How we swick against
            the long port home
      The lever how sliding and
            quarter bits with action
      A darling cut from trees
            If you insist come sorry
      Flight flurry or tongue
            lapping the sky we are
      The stirring nimbus pike
            and splip and the pull O
      the pull the sudden and
          slivering sovereignty
            the blistering breath
      nhhh
            frish   frish
nhhh

Ricki Mandeville

Nights I Can't Sleep, I Ride

Tall grass whispers around Ben's hooves, the moon
glows like the lit end of a cigarette, then sinks fast, as though

to stub itself out against the horizon. There's haze in the air tonight—
what Mama used to call fairy breath—that makes the prairie look blue.

This is the magic I come for when I leave my bed at night,
head for the barn in pajamas and boots. This is what I want

when I open the stall door, press my face into Ben's neck,
whisper Let's ride and slip astride: sage

that shimmers in clumps on the ground, balls of tumbleweed
waiting for a breeze to roll their pale bones

toward the barbed-wire fence. Land that stretches miles
ahead and behind, layers of history crumbled to rich, red dirt

that muffles our passage to a languid clop, clop as we ramble north.
The cobalt silence strokes my eyes like feathers.

His breath steams the air silver and there's no wind, even the grass
doesn't make a sound as it springs back up, erases our passage.

I'll doze in the saddle, let Ben turn back when he's ready,
sleep out the night in the barn on a pillow of sweet hay.

Angela Moore

Sweet Dreams

Sweet sugar spun dreams
Wrapped in jeweled webs
Clouds of lavender greens
Float above nightmares
Melt away as I awake
Leave me feeling stretchy
I yawn and turn to take a look

And jump when I see it's eight thirty

Jaimes Palacio

Donut Part 2

"What you're really asking them to admit is,
Oh my God, I don't really exist. I might be gone at any given second."
-Roger Ebert

The beautiful young Latin
girl sitting nearby with her
family is happily oblivious;
talking in excited Spanish, honestly
enjoying a night out. But he is not
really thinking of her. Not really
giving much attention to the glazed
donut he is treating himself to. The girl's
smile reminded him of someone he used
to be close to. Possibilities left to their
own demolition derby devices. Just
recently a beloved movie critic lost
his battle with Cancer. He thinks of an
old friend who also lost that battle. Thinks
of another friend who is fighting that battle.
Thinks of how he wished he could dismantle
it all. Build the world in a newer, crueless
state. But that would be playing God, and he
has trouble enough playing a man. He takes
another bite of the donut. It is a good
donut. He looks up into the nearly starless
sky. Somewhere, billions of miles past
his viewpoint, scientists discovered a place
so bright, they theorize the human brain could not
handle the colors. That anyone close enough
would go immediately insane. Some claim that this
place could be Heaven.

Angela Moore

Blue Heron

Draped over a boulder

The surface sears into my skin as my toes and fingers freeze in the Kern

Lulled by the sound of river around grey and wind through green

Cleansed by the scent of pine, drying mud and algae.

My eyelids flutter in time to see a pair of blue heron touch down on the bank.

Stilling my breath I inhale the sight

We are a trio of quiet

For sacred seconds until wings unfurl and lift

Taking my breath and leaving me saved.

Khadija Anderson

Cooper Creek

clouds are puffing messages at me
and a stellar jay is screaming them

I can hear the wind around me
but it is hiding

mumbling incoherently
never getting close enough

the flies are trying to whisper in my ears
but the trees won't say anything

the stream is full of clocks and barking dogs
and yelling people my husband says

it's just the voices of water spirits
but I swear it's someone I know

Julia Beasley

Blue Jay!

Blue Jay! Blue Jay!!
Where Could She be?
Blue Jay! Blue Jay!!
Where Could She be?
She Not in The Tree house
Not in The Caves
She Not in The Meadow
Where Could She be?

Where are You?
Blue Jay!!!

I saw Blue Jay on the ground
Covered in blood she was dead...............

Blue Jay You Who saved my life.
You Who saved my mind.
You Who saved my heart

Carrie McKay

Sequoia Immigration Studies

The roots of the cactus still remember,
the emerald lake cutting the buttes and
our braches that scraped the skyline.
When the sun was cool and then hot,
and rivers rose to settle the dust.

Stories passed down from branch to seed.
Dust and famine filled the sea and
pushed our people to the tall grey mountains.
We followed the men who gave us our name,
who spread our seed in the shade
and we grew strong and tall with their sons.

The creatures that soared and nested
are remembered in yellow stone;
but we are remembered in your pain.
Your rings are the family Bible
and you pass on our name with every tick
of the train over the track of your bones.

Lori McGinn

Half-Dome

Let us climb the face of half dome
Hold hands carefree as children
Teach our shadows to fly
Free fall into the violet sky

(For R.A.C.)

#1

When your mom killed you
She peeled your skin like an apple
cut your baby flesh up for a pie.
Ishtar, appeasing her Gods, gave you up for an offering.

She is the shadow in the corner
sucking the life from your bones
you are her fashion statement.

She is sporting new flesh colored shoes, with purse
and hat to match.
She walks out the door. Never looks back.

#2

Your heart was tossed to the dogs next door.
they licked it gently,
cried as dogs do.
carried it to their master.

He drapes his skin around your heart.
Gives you his breath,
Lays you in a field of hope and love.
Stands guard, stoic as a Masai warrior.

#3

I have cradled you
in my arms before
the world began

Such a question mark mouth
an effervescent brow
you are liquid spirit

Fire rests in your bones
you stand tall with attitude
belt buckle proud, with carved initials.

#4

All blues and hot breath your man came
a stealth bomber,
diving right to the dark
middle of you.
he had a library of books in his eyes.
he ate you right up.
You are resting inside him,
you are home.

#5

Family has a vanilla smell, delicious as a fresh baked right out of the oven cookie

#6

I have never looked down from the top of half-dome
Never climbed that high
But I can say my children have.
My heart stops every time I think of it.

Stefano Capobianco

True Love

Inside my Heart
There is a place
That struggles to find if true love has a face

What gives me hope
Hope seems so blind,
And where does one go when hope seems so hard to find

Every day is an endless search
For something so undefined
So how could anyone believe that peace will come in time

Somewhere there's love
Love that's kind and true
But in these times it's all too often not the rule

Every day is an endless search
For something so undefined
So how could anyone believe that peace will come in time

It's all been said
The words are dead
But in these arms, you'll find I've got so much to give
In these arms, you'll find I've got so much to give

Emma McGinn

Love Is…

Love Is…
A powerful tide
That pulls you
into a gigantic hug.
Love is seeing my dad
again. Love is when I
dance around the room
With my mom. Love is
me Laughing with my
brother. The greatest
love there is, the love
that lets me share my
name with my family.

Satyajit Mayadas

I love you more then anything

I love you more then burritos, chocolate marzipan and Doritos.
I love you more then orange juice, sourdough pancakes, and c
I love you more then sunflower seeds, my last name Mayadas and baked beans.
I love you more then baseballs, chocolate bars and racecars.
I love you more then karate baseball players and Pilates.
And as you can see I love you more then anything.

Maggie Ambrose

A Love Poem

I love you more than pancakes,
And beef taquitos,
And Fritos.

I love you more than birthday cake,
Caramel apples,
And really rare steak.

I love you more than softball,
And Nana's apple pies,
And the Friday Fish Frys.

I love you more than my new house,
Than Disneyland ,
And Mickey Mouse.

I love you more than a chicken,
Than homemade ice cream,
And Ripstikin'.
I like bacon a ton,
But you are my favorite one.

Adem Oygur

The Chicken and the Mouse

A Truck was carrying a duck
A fox was in a box
A sheep was driving a jeep.
We all went to Mouse's house
For cookies, tea, and milk.

Nursultan Oygur

Planting a Garden

I have a very beautiful garden.
It was boring while I was planting.
But mom said I was hardworking.
The brown soil got me dirty,
but it was worth it when I saw the pretty flowers…
The fruits and vegetables were so tasty.
I love you plants.
I like caring for you and watching you grow through your little lifetime.

JL Martindale

Aunt Otter's Garden

Bougainvillea devours the crumbling walls of the 1918 cottage.
The woody vines, gnarled and twisted like Aunt Otter's fingers, reach
impossibilities while the elderly woman sits, contented breathing
in her old wicker chair.
Her rusty watering can, like her fog-filled mind, waits, patiently,
for the green tendrils to embrace it, fill it, bring it to the dark brambles
and warm moist earth of forever night,
forever life.

Ken Schmidt

Oohhhh, I get it

I have a plant

That lives out on my patio

In a pot, over by the climbing Rose Bush

It is about 6 feet tall

A False Aralia

It is always falling over

Every time it falls over, dirt falls out of the pot and onto the patio

I always go over and set the plant up again

But still the dirt is out of the pot and on the patio

The plant does this a lot

Pretty soon almost all of the dirt is out of the pot

Then I go over, set the plant up, and put new potting soil into the pot,

And everything is back as it should be.

The plant has started doing this again

Falling over, spilling it's dirt,

The plant and the root ball are now almost completely out of the pot

It always takes the drip watering hose with it

Only this morning did I realize . . . .

The plant is trying to escape.

Emme O'Toole

A Journal's Entry

I was going to be there,
feeling the wind as the tractor
rides off into the patches of vegetables
I would've helped her record her favorite plants,
all the information she learned that day,
I was going to make the trip educational.
I would've chilled with the cabbage,
flirted with the strawberries
and laughed with the watermelon.
The corn would've recognized me,
but I would've forgotten her name,
therefore ignoring her.
We would've smelled the freshly mowed grass,
the dirty new soil
and the sweat of everyone there.
We were going to be tourists together,
traveling the world
- well, the farm -
and forever remember the memories
of that day because she had written them in me.
But no, she had to leave me on the table
the pen still behind her ear,
walking away thinking she was prepared for the day.
I wanted to shout out to her,
remind her of all the memories
we were going to make
but now they're just memories that will never be created,
never be written inside of me,
never be shared and laughed about
by her and I together.
Now they are memories that will never be made
because of a
forgetful memory
and a non-existent mouth.

Maggie Ambrose

Four Chickens in a Coop

Four chickens in a coop.
One was black and white.
Her name is Zebra
And she likes to peck and bite.
This is Queen.
She's black,
Or green,
Or in between.
Next is Sunny, a yellow, mellow fellow.
Now here you are, Cutie.
Cutie is nice and she loves to eat rice.
Here are four chickens in a coop.

Omer Oygur

The Bird is Flying

The bird is flying
The dragon is breathing fire
The Sun is shining
The frog is jumping
The dolphins are swimming.
The fish is hunting
The minnow dies.

Benci Udovch Gottdank

The Interesting Pretending Objects

The phone pretended to be a remote control and flew the helicopter to Mars.

The windmill pretended to be a shuriken and cut down the tree.

The magnifying glass pretended to be a bubble wand and blew bubbles all about.

The castle pretended to be a rook and won the board game of chess.

The alien laser shooter pretended to be a word bubble and was in the comic book.

The plane pretended to be a jet and to go super fast.

The dice pretended to be a office building and people went to work there.

The smiley face pretended to be a bubble to float up high.

Satyajit Mayadas

The Round Rainbow Bubble

A clear, magic crystal ball
floating in the air,

It sees me in my writing class,
writing about it.

It sees the little kids playing
hide-and-seek in the park behind me.

It sees the big, red tomatoes
growing bigger by the minute,
Almost touching the ground.

It sees the green okra
and bell peppers in my colorful garden.

It feels my gaze on it,
and then poof,
it's gone.

Kathryn Claudi-Magnussen

What color am I?

What color am I?
I love Halloween and I smell like pumpkin butter. I taste like candy corn, and creamsicles.
I look like mars. I sound like fire, and I feel like a football.

What color am I?
I look like mud and sound like rustling leaves. I smell like rich soil, chocolate chip cookies, and coffee cake. I taste like hot cocoa, brownies, and a cracked open coconut. I feel like squishy clay, soft fur, tree bark, and pine cones. I am relaxed and happy!

What color am I?
I look like clover and tree leaves.
I smell like spring, mint, and limes.
I sound like a growing garden, rain forests, and bushes rustling in the wind.
I taste like lettuce, cucumbers, honeydew melon, and sweet peas.
I feel like grass and it makes me lucky!

What color am I
I look like darkness and shadows.
I sound like thunder and howling wolves.
I smell like burnt toast.
I taste like licorice and cola.
I feel like velvet and ice.
It makes me feel mysterious and invisible..............

What color am I?
I look like valentines and hearts.
I smell like roses and bubble gum.
I sound like pigs.
I taste like watermelon and cotton candy.
I feel like ballerina tutus.
I am loving, lively, and sweet.

What color am I?
I look like daisies in the sun light.
I smell like a birthday baking in the oven.
I sound like fluttering butterflies in the wind.
I taste like a piece of golden brown cake.
I feel like a soft piece of silk.
I am warm and happy!!

Daniel McGinn

The Color of Cody

Cody had never seen colors.
Cody opened his eyes on the day he was born, and he could not see.
The world was white and white was the color in Cody's eyes.

Cody knew his room was yellow,
his mother had told him that his blankets were yellow,
the walls were yellow,
even the flowers outside of his window were yellow,
the sun was yellow.
Cody knew what yellow felt like.
Yellow was warm.

Orange.
Orange was the color of morning.
Cody drank orange juice, every day, with breakfast.
Cody knew what orange tasted like.

Purple was a fast color in Cody's mind,
the family car was purple,
purple grapes were quick and round,
Cody liked to roll them on the kitchen floor,
but purple doesn't bounce, purple is wet, and squishy.

Cody went to the ocean once,
the ocean is as blue as a swimming pool,
the sky is blue,
blue is a big color,
blue is a color you can swim in,
blue makes you want to fly.

Cody's mother gave him a dollar,
it was green, it was dry as the grass
and it made his fingers itch.
Cody spent his green dollar.

It fell from his hand like a leaf from a tree.
Green is a pretty color, but it doesn't last long.

Cody has a red whistle,
red is a loud color like a fire engine,
things that are red happen suddenly,
like when somebody gives you a candied apple at a surprise party.
Red is so sweet it makes you smile.

Somebody told Cody that people have colors.
Cody began to wonder. "What color am I?"
Cody asked his mother, "What color am I?"
and this is what she told him...

"You are red and sweet and you make me smile.
You are the green grass and better than money.
You are blue as an ocean and open as the sky.
You are purple and fast but bouncy too.
You are orange like juice in the breakfast tummy.
You are yellow and warm like the sun in my window.

You are all of these colors,
you are every color you have ever known,
that's what color you are,
and nobody else is the color of Cody."

That's what Cody's mother says.

Luke Salazar

Mother

acquiesced one day, and bought the lonely six-year-old a grey fluffy kitten. It slept on her bed, she felt love's gauzy touch for the first time. One day, she took her kitten outside for a walk. It never came back. She was six -- how could she know? When their drafty old house would sway and creak, the girl imagined the ghost of the kitten, padding amongst the dead halls.

At seven, she found a dollar in the pocket of her thrift store dress. Bought a white mouse at the local pet store. Just a feeder, so the clerk didn't ask. She made a little bed for it… in her dresser drawer. She was seven -- how could she know? But at least she would spot it occasionally, a blur of white in the kitchen, opposed to the blurs of dark grey.

At eight, she bought a goldfish. She put it in a cereal bowl by her bed, came home from school to find it dead on the floor, having leapt from the bowl's shallow lip. Every time the plumbing groaned, she could hear it burbling deep beneath the house.

At nine, Mother (sick of all the break-ins) got a dog for defense. The girl wanted to love it, tolerated the flea bites all over her legs, but the next time burglars cleaned them out of their meager possessions, the dog was found cowering under the couch in terror. It took days to coax him out. She was old enough not to believe about the farm in the countryside. The dog was gone, but at least the fleas stuck around.

At ten, she discovered "Free to Good Home," sat with pen and Pennysaver at the kitchen table, looked for addresses within bicycle range. Always to be confronted with the same question she'd so often asked herself:

"Where's your mom?"

Nicholas Stephen

Collective Epiphanies

Cobblestones are burning beneath the street lights.
They say
we're walking with too much friction.
We need to be cool.
The sky is choking clouds
and making faces at me.
Stop pretending to be and
just be.
We've already seen WHO you can be,
now, just be YOU.

As if trying to make more space for something
the traffic rearranges itself.
The streets have no idea what merging is
and the singing birds have not yet learned
that fire sirens aren't
their brethren's calls returned.

I told you there was something here
and laughing you twirled sunlight around your finger.
You painted the air with presence,
I still have trouble breathing.
If you put your ear against my chest
you can hear the ocean in my lungs
rising to the pull of your moonlight skin.
Your
gravity.

You laugh at me
when I tell you nice things.
That's why I do.

I get so lost sometimes but
I almost know where I am again.

You catch me in your Rubix-kaleidoscopic eyes
and whisper under your breath,
THIS IS JUST THE BEGINNING
EVEN IF IT'S THE END OF SOMETHING ELSE.

I wanted you to know,
it wasn't always this beautiful.

You helped me notice.

Flocks of crayon colored static drips from stereo speakers.
Beings caught between frequencies.
Broadcasted solitude in-between radio stations.

A daydream is stuck in your head
as you hum a song
no one has ever heard.
Where did you learn to bend notes so beautifully?
You laugh at me again,
honestly.
We must have traveled here in a pensive hourglass.
The sand spinning like a halcyon tornado in our sleep,
saying,
TAKE YOUR TIME.
YOU DESERVE IT.

I forget things easily
so be patient with me, please,
because within this place, you hold
all collective epiphanies.

I KNOW I'M GOING TO WAKE SOON.

I close my eyes and wait for eternal to pass.
I can smell rain.
As each moment echoes off our breath like reverb
all seven billion hearts beat at once and everything stops.
I feel your hand close around mine,
I hear you breathe to say something,

I open my eyes,
and everything
stops.

Emme O'Toole

I am the Title of your Book

I am the title of you're book,
the bird of your tree that sings
in the early morning,
the answer to your question
I am the Shepard dog of your sheep,
the clouds and day light streaming
in from your bedroom window
I am the thunder
you are the lightning
I am that one special star
for you to wish on every night
I am the gold from your rainbow
that everyone chases after
I am the light from your hearth fire,
I am the numbers for your dice
You are nothing without me
I make you complete.

G. Murray Thomas

"Your Kidney Just Arrived At Lax"

The doctor told me as I lay in pre-op prep.
I envisioned a special chartered flight,
an entire airplane filled with organs.

Hearts with little heart shaped carry-ons.
They always watch the inflight movie
and cry all the way through.

Livers splurging on one last drink;
they don't think they'll be allowed
where they're going.

The lungs eye the spot
where the oxygen masks drop.

Corneas stare out at the passing countryside;
they always get a window seat.

The spleens are always complaining
    about security
    about the length of the flight
    about the lack of leg room
    (although they have no legs).

The gall bladder always gets in line
before his row is called.

And there's my kidney,
no doubt reading a book to pass the time
something classic: As I Lay Dying,
    or Great Expectations,
    or The Stranger.

All of them wondering
about the journey ahead,
about their new home,
about their new life.

Eric Lawson

Airplane Cruises Towards a Crack in the Window Pane

I see the airplane, tiny, distant, quiet, unassuming,
appear at the far left of the giant window pane.
Though I know it's unlikely, I wonder if you're on it.
Jet-setting off to some gallery opening or island.
To the
far right,
I see the spider web crack that is splintering
the glass a little more each day, branching out.
Does the 727 see the giant crack looming ahead?
Surely the pilot knows this means certain doom.
I wonder if you ever consider window pane cracks
in all your comings and goings, your frequent flyer.
I'm not sure
if it's reflex, disdain or genuine concern,
but I place my hand upon the window,
on top of the crack, as if it erase it from view.
Don't see the crack, pilot!
Don't fly into the imperfection!
Don't take from me the one I love!
Don't force me to use exclamation points!
The the
far right,
I see the plane emerge beneath my hand.
Crisis overted.
Life goes on.
I am still here, pretending not to be bored.
You are still there, boarding another plane.

Martha Jeanne Stothard

The Lonely Moon

The man in the moon was thinking one day
"What shall I do, what shall I say?"
I'm here all alone, I haven't a friend.
No one to share with.
Oh! How will it end?"
The poor old moon, he needed a friend,
Some one to talk to, someone to defend.
He had an idea " A planet I'll find,
One that is lonely, one that is kind."
He looked over here, he looked over there
But he could not find one that was even aware.
"I will not give up, I need a friend,
I'll search the universe to its very end."
He saw many a world,
He spoke to them all but they'd just depart.
He was always left with his lonely heart.
Then one day in the far, far away,
A little speck of a place was shinning it's day.
He spoke to her, she answered back.
Now Earth and Moon have an eternal pact.

Nursultan Oygur

Queen of The Clouds

Birdina is queen of the clouds
Her job is to keep the clouds moving
When she breaths she makes a soft breeze.
In her spare time she likes to talk to her fellow bids
But more than anything
She wants to play a joke on the goddess of cats.
She is not very good at being truthful
But she is always nice.

Ella Hayes

I Am A Black Cat

I am a black cat slinking along on the street,
Waiting for a mouse.
I wonder if the mouse will come soon.
I hear the mouse squeak and I attack.
I want chocolate.
I imagine that I am eating the mouse.
The mouse tastes so good!
I feel the mouse's blood seep into my stomach.
Ouch! The blood burns!
I am a black cat and I am sorry I ate that mouse.
I understand that I should never eat a mouse ever again.
I say! I did not eat a mouse! I just dreamed about it!
I tried to eat it, but I missed!
Ouch! The blood burns again!
I think I will die.
I am a black cat wishing that I would die.

Neela

Rock Star Cheetah

Rock Star Cheetah was mean.
She was as mean as a cat.
She was meaner than a cat,
she was as mean as a cheetah.
She howled at the crowd.
She purred to the audience.
She ran around the stage really fast.
But there was one thing she couldn't do though...Roar!
She couldn't roar!

Collin Moore

Do I Remember...

A simple question
Once and for all
Do I remember
Learning to play baseball?

I remember my cousin
Who would ask to play the sport
I would hit hard and run
He would always say he was done

I remember my dad
He would get me all my gear
And everybody would cheer
About all the bases I just cleared

I remember my Coach Glen
He would put me in positions
I played many of them and I was scattered
He made me 4th and I was flattered

I remember the playoffs
Our team got first place
We won the World Series too
And it seemed that I was an ace

A simple question
Once and for all
Do you remember
Learning to play baseball?

Alison

The Riddler

If you are walking down Manhattan Lane in Manhattan, New York, at 5 o'clock pm, you will find everyone rushing indoors. The kindest people will take you into their homes until 5:30 pm, and the less kind will just grab you and drag you in. For, coming down the lane, is The Riddler.

He has no body, and his voice seems to come from everywhere at once. If he catches you, he will ask of you a riddle. If you get the riddle wrong... Well, we don't really know what happens, for two reasons. 1. Everyone hides from him. 2. He (hopefully) doesn't catch anyone. Still, no-one is willing to find out, especially since brave, young Peter Hamilton decided to chance a meeting with The Riddler at age 19.

Now, people say that he should've listened to his elders, should've gone inside like everyone else. But, as the story goes, Peter stayed outside, and, as everyone hid themselves away, confronted The Riddler. He was asked, "How can a pants pocket be empty and still have something in it?". He answered with, "It can have a hole in it". Ultimately, Mr. Peter Hamilton was never heard from again.

Some think he was turned into the cat that follows The Riddler everywhere, but his fate may not have been that serene...

Matt Foster

The Impossible

Enter a world of superheroes
and ripped people
who are all attractive

Save the world
One nemesis at a time.
Almost like a utopia,
very peaceful.
Imagine our world
different than now.

A dream for a perfect
world,
sounds impossible.
They say

Michael Cantin

Cretaceous Carnivore, Cantankerous

A terrible roar shakes the unsuspecting earth
Driving tiny mammal-like creatures to flee
to the safety of dank burrows.
Heavy set herd beasts cut their meals short to listen.
Feathered pack hunters snap and chirp at one another.
It is difficult to ignore the obvious.

The Tyrant Lizard King is perturbed.
(All of his friends call him "Rex")
He stomps his massive triple toed feet:
his talons alone spelling death for those below.
A scavenger looks up,
paralyzed in a Godzilla movie scream,
and is crushed underfoot.

Teeth gnash violently.
saliva is flung into trees.
Vestigial limbs stretch out in desperation,
the atrophied memories of arms.
For the first time, the Predator King whines.
This sensation is driving him mad.
His tail lashes in a toddler's fit.

This itch he cannot hope to reach,
and none are fool enough to help him scratch.

Greg Patrick

Dragon's Own.
To Usurp the Night's Throne

"Riddle. A box without hinges, key, or lid yet golden treasure inside is hid." -Don Tolkien

Prompt: "I was born"…

a hatchling dragon, the smoldering ember of an inferno, like a red tree's seed germinating. Coiled around her brood the massive wings like those of an eagle guarding her aeire. The dragoness shielding her young from marauding knights. The simmering flames illuminate the hoard of an emperor's ransom in precious gems like a sea of fire smoldering. The tribute of the ancients offered by the shamans and druids of the old peoples and ways. Till men came over the sea with iron and flame and new ways and her people came no more to offer her homage and the darkness filled the void again.

She preyed not upon maid, man, nor herd but drew sustenance as if from roots or gold veins into the earth, basking on the great splendour dais of silver and emerald. A nest of transparent embryos of the eggs and the young dragons within before darkness again fills the cavern.

Like transluscent chryssalus' of fire they are. A firefly in a jar each seems. In suspended animation incubating like antediluvian creatures in amber formations. Like the specimens of an alchemist's labratory, an animus in each vial it seemed or the dark prediction of a Roma's divination orb. A realm of dark dreams and poetry.

Like an ember in a hearth a knight-errant appears at the threshold, silhouetted against the torch-light and stars, his shadow cast long and ominously. A bogeyman of a fledging dragonling's nursery. The only true monster a dragon knows. Dismounted for his horse shied away from the fiery portal into the mountain-side. With deceptive languidity the dragoness does not stir. Her lidless gaze alone betrays the age-old vigilance, young when none akin to the shape of man walked these flood and fire-shaped lands. A fire that never sleeps begins to kindle within her heart even as the mountain's flames are dormant.

The torch seems like the summer sun of a new dawn awakening a great beast from hibernation. He draws his sword, expecting it's scales to adorn his shield or helm. The glacial sheen of blade mirrors in the dragon's eye like a silver candle flame, it's eye dilates and contracts at the torch's glare. Like a pool of phosphorous it seems. Balefire microcosmed glares in reply. As proportionate in size as rearing cobra to a mouse, the two adversaries appraised each-other. Her sigh is as if the purr of many tigresses. Instead of the acclaim he anticipated, the dragon's roar fills the world and imagination. Like the battle cry of an ancient titan, the groan of Atlas, world-bearer.

The cavern walls shudder as if in fear. The dragon rears it's serpentine countenance then taloned wings flaring protectively like maelstrom-billowed canvases and scaled thorax expanding. As the knight advances his battlecry is drowned out by the immense roar of the dragon, deafening in the confines of what seems a subterranean cathedral.

Stalactites fall like spears around him. His shield upraised to avoid the geologic shards. It seemed the earth itself roared in defiance. A primal instinct to defend one's own and innocent that has been lost so long on modern man in his world of iron and stone. His own smoking dragon castles that burn the world and sky. Like the groan of an entire munition's factory the dragon's breath he feels like a crusade's sun beating down on him. Then he feels as if he is soaring as teeth lock on his armour-clad form. No more can it withstand than a scavenging beatle's exoskeleton to a raven. And he is raised and cast down. To a pile of blades and armour. Like moths drawn to a promethean flame. The squire cowers and flees. He is left to do so. Then a writhing shudder of comprehension as she realized an egg was stolen.

Silhouetted against the moon like a chimeric heraldry emblazoned, hers was a battlecry of fire, her shadow cast like that of a raptor upon her fleeing quarry below. The black-robed shamans of the new peoples believed that her species were fallen or rebel angels that took refuge in the depths. So it nigh seemed if one ascertained essence by guise alone for she descended like a burning star upon the turrets of a castle overlooking the countryside. The serfs who toiled below welcomed the sight with tearful gaiety for the ancient prophecy that the dragon would rise at their hour of need from the hollow hills to liberate the subjugated from the oppression of their new overlords, seemed realized. She left them unscathed and their hopes seemed rekindled and confirmed when a line of men at arms arrayed to hold her at bay were incinerated as their spear casts glanced harmlessly of her scales. The portcullis and drawbridge closed just as a gaping maw opened and flame enveloped the walls like a Vesuvian fury befalling empire.

Like a great Amazonian serpent her coils encircled the keep crushing masonry like a quarry's ribcage. Like a taloned hand wrenching a chesspiece she tore the tower and battlements from the foundations. The egg was cast from the turret and she caught it in mid-flight. The shell cracked open and like a phoenix reborn from ash the young dragon breathed it's first of the night air, her firesong's crooning lulled it to repose and she sheltered it under membraned wings like the ceiling of a gothic cathedral. Sanctuary to the innocent against the sword. Wings enfolded over protectively as if tucked into the pages of legend like bedcovers of a rune-cast slumber.

With a contented sigh like a tempest wave of molten silver subsiding and fires cooled like magma or mountain's thaw pervading her she descends back to her slumber. The fire-encrimsoned forest seem like palatial torches of an ancient sylvan bastion as if midday shines by eve till the new dawn banishes all dragons from mind. And in the dark where dragon's sleep and bards compose, people learn to dream again

Khadija Anderson

Super Chief

The other day I started to write a poem about my father. When he was a boy, he rode Southern Pacific Railroad's Super Chief train every summer from California to Chicago to visit his father. Once at the train stop in Albuquerque he bought two Pueblo tourist wedding vases for my grandmother. She had them on her kitchen counter all through my childhood. 70 years after my father bought the smooth matte vases with the geometric designs, the colors are still vivid from the bright colored paint used for tourist pots instead of earth toned plant based paints for everyday pots. The vases are in my kitchen now.

Today I walked into a bookstore and while passing some greeting cards one caught my eye. Covering the card were geometric designs drawn in shades of brown and rust and ocher. In the bottom corner of the drawing was a small train coming out of a tunnel heading into another tunnel leading into a wall of geometric designs of maize, plowed fields, and shields with feathers. On the back of the card was the title of the drawing: "Super Chief".

Ricki Mandeville

My Father's Hands

You have your father's hands
my mother would say, tucking the words
into the pockets and hems of my childhood.

I do—my fingers long and tapered like his.
But his cut out cancers, stitched severed tissue,
stopped bleeding, closed wounds.

Mine, on the other hand, write poems
about hands I haven't held, poems about
an earnest face in sepia, framed on the mantel.

Poems about stopping the bleeding, poems
about closing the wounds that carve themselves into us,
that we wear like scars or badges.

Like the moment I first met my father. I was twenty-four.
He was at the quiet meeting place long ahead of me.
It was early spring, but cold, my coat long enough

to cushion my knees as I knelt beside the stone.
Hello, Father, I said, pressing my hands, SO LIKE HIS,
against the cold marble.

Stephanie Jones

He never did

The first time he tried to teach me to drive stick
I crumbled over the steering wheel
chest heaving as though an earthquake
had pried open my ribcage,
my lungs having too much space to breathe.

He told me:
"It's okay, I'm not mad. I'm not going to yell at you. I'm not your father".

22 years of living,
my father never once called me,
"Beautiful".
So when people get love-drunk on the newness of me
and tell me how precious I am,
I fear they'll want to be my father,
pour cements in the cracks he left on my heart
but it's hard to need something you've never had.

Before anyone tries to place themselves into the
holes where I will never heal right,
I tell them this story:

Before permanence touched the reach of memory,
when I barely tall enough to reach kneecaps,
there is a picture of my father putting me on the kitchen table,
wiping frosting off my mouth.
I am giggling,
all baby teeth and bare gums.
My father still has hair,
he's still young and kind.
Sometimes then I imagine he called me beautiful.

Seth Halbeisen

Sadness is Bad

If hope can set you free,
And worry is an annoying biting flea.
Fear is just an instigator,
with Anger an insinuator,
Then it can only be,
That sadness is bad.

If grief is just a well,
that leads all the way to hell,
And despair is a locked prison cell,
Then their root must be as well.
Mathematics can surely tell,
That sadness is bad.

If you heart woefully bleeds,
Torn apart by a hundred dead trees.
And the pain is more than you can bear,
Has you thinking of poking a bear.
Please remember this reading,
For soon you to will be seeing.
That sadness is bad.

If the world has pulled you down,
Shaped your face into a frown.
And you think your ready for more,
Please don't open up that door.
Just let these feelings go,
For surely you to must know.
That sadness is so very...
So soul devouringly scary.
So unbelievably sedentary.
So terribly unnecessary.
Surely you must agree,
That sadness is bad.

Betsy Mars

Inflammatory

Burned out at twenty
T(w)(o)o
(l)ate/8 with no spirit
no fight
left

to look for love

NO
Strangers
Shooting questions, like stars,
bear the answers
bare the answers
barely answers

or none at all

Burned out at twenty
No words or rhythms
Nothing to make this mood
Worthwhile

No sense to sensitivity
No meaning to misery
No art to arthritis
of the mind and motion.

Stiff bones of non-pursuit
caught feet in dead tracks
tracts of grassmud
gripping feet

Displaced
Standing still in brittle

bones of fear
of non-reflection
self-rejection
Will crush(ed)

Stagnant
in arthritic
bones of definitions, self-restriction
Make no bones about it:
Stagnant down
deeper
into self with
drawn in questions,
black tight-laced yawns.

Fatigue of avoidance
A void dance
Plays on words and rhymes to fill
the
empty
SPACE:
The final front/(t)ear.

Daniel McGinn

Now that I'm Sixty

I can learn to say I'm sorry
I would rather dance with you than run from you

Look at me
Look at all these things I still have to do

Children are more than background noise
Children are like the ocean

The neighbors run off to work
I'm so happy I never killed anybody

I spill my guts to the ripe red tomatoes
Every time a mother dies all the babies cry

Children are more than mirrors
Children are more than anything

Sweet talk the white flowers
Marvel at the strawberries

Children are more than an echo
Every little thing makes ripples

Thea Iberall

The recipe

For Marion Neuberger (1919-2012)

I remember how she taught me to make potato latkes.
In the small kitchen, I towered over her like a skyscraper.
Cut the potatoes lengthwise and grate, she explains.
Salt, two eggs, pepper. Get rid of the juice and add
an onion and matzo meal until thick. Spoon
into a sizzling frying pan. Loosen the bottoms.

We hold hands, ready to say the Chanukah prayer. Marion
can't find the real candles so we scurry our little circle over
to the blue fake electric ones in the window and chant
backdropped by a Christmas-lit street filled with strings
of white snowflakes, red candy canes and orange angels.

At the table, we eat from plates piled with latkes and roasted
chicken and snap peas. Marion pulls out an album from her trip
to Krakow. We stare at her pictures from Auschwitz as she
points to the stacks of shoes, the mounds of glasses, the heaps
of human hair. Her eyes are soft and big. She murmurs, it was
the case with one child's undershirt where I began to cry.

In the backyard of the board-and-care, she spends her last
birthday with her friends sitting under a box elder tree.
The four of them, white-haired and wrinkled, trade dirty jokes
like baseball cards. Together they've lived 374 years, one
has a wheelchair, another a walker, another a cane. The oldest
walks on her own. Marion can't remember a punch line. She points
to her friend and laughs, my brains are in her head.

On New Year's Eve, the activity director asks her to list
some resolutions. Marion is wearing a golden crown, her hair
hasn't been done up in days. Her head is bent, her eyes
bloodshot. The Christmas tree behind her is eight feet tall. Someone

took one of the popcorn strands and placed it around her neck. I want to learn to crochet, she whispers, and then, get a job.

RD Armstrong

Corizon

Passion
lives inside
the sweaty folds
of mingling
bodies

But

The origins
of passion are
hidden away
from our
insatiable
curiosity,
our crazy
need to know.

THE HEART IS A LONELY HUNTER
THE HUNTER IS A LONELY HEART
LONELY IS THE HEART HUNTER
HEART IS THE LONELY HUNTER

Cynthia Quevedo

But For A Home

He's not cold
he has thick walls
encasing his heart.

His soul lays
inside
waiting for something

it doesn't quite remember.

Like one cancer cell

anticipating it's moment
to multiply.

If we could figure
out cancer,

maybe

we can figure love out too.

Ruth Blue

Mind

My mind is a forest fire.
There are no tourists here.
It's all clear.
Fear hides inside It's box.
Thoughts talk and talk.
Memories flow out like lava.
As the life of this mind goes on and on.

Thea Iberell

Orejas de Elephante

Dedicated to Eloisa Saucedo (1952-2010)

When an elephant is dying, the rest of the herd gathers round,
stands by as if concerned, gently nudging her
face and limbs with their trunks making sounds as if
agonized as if knowing about impermanence and passages.
They forage for food then return to their vigil to nudge
and pace in the moonlight, knead the dying one's head,
bring leaves for her bed as if their cheeks flatten with grief
and their bellies thud dull. And then later, they bring
the bones of the dead back home, a piled geology of
eye sockets and long femurs and they curl above
her unmasked drumbeat as if their hearts
are splintering like wood chips and their dreams
circle between fierceness and fear.

So now as I sit beside Eloisa's hospital bed, her head thrust
back, neck muscles cross from ear to clavicle like a ballerina
in pose. Machines click her heart beat, her breath rasps slow.
Lupe returns from the cafeteria to comb out her sister's
once beautiful hair. She whispers of Zacatecas growing up,
the time a neighborhood boy threw a rock, the first time
the sisters skipped down to the *panaderia* for elephant
ear pastries with cinnamon and pecans. Now tubes
intertwine her arms, family members gather, they pace
and nudge. Outside, the full moon looms large on the horizon.
We turn her every two hours, add extra pillows to soften the bed.

When I think about death, I think about the elephants. When
I think about death I think about the bones.

Betsy Mars

Pole Dancing

The two poles of my existence,
father and son.
In the middle, the equator,
flat-lining.
The earth revolves off-balance
and shifts
as needs demand.

Aquarian, the water bearer,
struggles to stay level.
The poles tip, seesawing,
(as) a tsunami threatens
the almost tranquil
shores of domesticity
my complicity
demands

 dam, be damned.

Don Kingfisher Campbell

The World Is

(1) *A Jungle*

mountains like
backs of
green leopards

little rectangle
houses are
colorful bugs
on land skin

a pride of
white fluffy
lions races
through ocean sky

but they
don't leave
brown dust in
exhausted air

it's rolling
gnats that
dully exhale

(2) *A Church*

from tiny ribbon
highway on flat horizon
downtown manuments
hundreds of times
smaller than

daily massive

white cloud
beings created to
occasionally grace
ants with tears

in return micro
creatures compost
poems in praise
of manifestations

of god force

Nicholas Steffen

Distance

The roads are viscous in the daylight.
I get lost in the distance
trying not to measure my journeys
in time or in miles.
I measure them in song lengths.
On any given day
you could be six punk rock songs away.
And I still find reasons not to go to you.

The place you go to heal
it will resemble your deepest wound.
All brick, bourbon and pyre.
You've got your hands so full of grief that you can't even hold your fire.
I'd need only look for the place that smells of your inferno.

Don't think for a second that I mind burning for you.
It's the distance that bothers me.

Leanne and Katie Hunt

Mother and Daughter Acrostics Fly across Sky and Kitchen Table

I. Fly

Frantic
Leapings into a
Yellow sky.

Fragile
Legs
Yo-yoing in my dinner.

II. Sky

Scorching
Unimaginably hot
No snow

III. Moon

Midnight's lamp shining for a million modern insomniacs tossing and rolling in tangled sheets.
Orchestrator of ocean tides and choreographer of cavorting ships and sea creatures.
One-sided orbiting partner in an eon-spanning dance of incrementally changing speeds and distance.
Nightlight for generations of children waking from nightmare into darkness.

Stephanie Jones

Rest

This is how the dust settles:

I.
when the wind tires of turning
sand grains for answers,
the wind becomes a dry heave of breath,
a wave void of water
until it gives in to its own thirst
and HUSH.
This gorgeous surrender
is as natural and unforgiving as aging
and the sun blankets the world in fire
before bursting into citrus plumes.

II.

when I am the only pair of shuffling ankles,
this city of rust carries me in its womb
when the darkness howls back.
The night is such a ferocious lover,
with its helicopter lips,
and its cricket legs
serenading me with its train throat.
The way its halo stars
give some god a shape.

III.

The stale air called out from my throat
so I heat scrawled "water" into the ground
but the flood never came.
Instead the earth turns itself slower,
slower in this darkness.

Such a soothing weight placed on my chest,
like the train's horn
        an exclamation point
cutting a silhouette of sound through this city of rust.
In its echo, it stained the night
whispering to me.

Acknowledgements:

Thank you to my wonderful and supportive family,
For The Love of Words Workshop Writers,
Deanne Brown, Daisy Chain, SOCHS, Jaimes Palacio,
Daniel & Lori McGinn, Ken Schmidt,
Alexis Tan, Cheng Cheng Tan,
Paul and everyone at It's a Grind.
Phil and The Ugly Mug and
Punxsutawney Phil—
who reminds me that everyday
is a new opportunity do it all again, better.

www.ingramcontent.com/pod-product-compliance
Lightning Source LLC
Chambersburg PA
CBHW020902090426
42736CB00008B/464